DISN

Barbara Ender-Jones

JPMGUIDES

Contents

- Sharing a dream 3
- Once upon a time 8
- Disneyland Park 11
- Walt Disney Studios Park 33
- Disney Village 44
- Shopping 45
- Dining out 50
- Hotels 56
- Golf Disneyland 63
- The hard facts 64
- Index 70

Maps
- Overview 6–7
- Disneyland Park 12–13
- Main Street, U.S.A. 14
- Frontierland 18
- Adventureland 22
- Fantasyland 24
- Discoveryland 28
- Walt Disney Studios Park 34–35
- Hotels 58–59
- How to get there 64

sharing a dream

The magic begins to work as soon as you walk through the gates. Something in the air lifts you into a world of make-believe, full of excitement and happy smiles – and no one seems the slightest bit embarrassed to wander around in a jester's hat with tassels on, a Goofy cap or a pair of plastic Mickey Mouse ears.

When Walt Disney first drew up the plans for a theme park in the 1950s, he wanted to create a place where parents could enjoy themselves as much as the children. And what was the secret ingredient in his magic potion? Something to wake up the child in every adult. His genius can't be denied: his sense of perfectionism and meticulous attention to detail are still respected by his successors today. Could he have imagined, when he dreamed up the personality of Mickey Mouse back in 1928, that the sophisticated kids of the digital era would wait in line for his autograph?

Based on the model of its American predecessors, the Disneyland Park at Marne-la-Vallée is divided into five interconnected "lands", designed on specific themes, taken up and developed in the rides and music, restaurants, shops and services, even in the trees and flowers. Fantasyland, for the smaller children, draws on fairy tales such as *Sleeping Beauty, Snow White, Cinderella* and

Sharing a dream

BEHIND THE SCENES

Hidden from view is a complete working city, with its own maintenance and construction workshops, warehouses, security department, and the largest costume wardrobe in Europe. Coming from all over the world, the 12,200 Cast Members represent more than 100 nationalities and 500 professions. There are 700 actors and dancers, 50 musicians, 150 designers and decorators, and 30 dressmakers to confect those fantastic costumes.

other childhood favourites like *Pinocchio*, *Peter Pan* and *Alice in Wonderland*. Frontierland is forts and cannons, cowboys, Indians and tales of the Gold Rush. Adventureland relives stories of *Swiss Family Robinson*, swashbuckling pirates, Ali Baba and Indiana Jones. Science fiction and the futuristic visions of Jules Verne were the inspiration of Discoveryland.

Since its creation in 1992, the park has become the most popular tourist destination in Europe. To celebrate its 10th anniversary, a second theme park, the Walt Disney Studios Park, opened in March 2002. The whole complex, including hotels, entertainment village and golf course became a fully fledged resort, under the new name Disneyland Resort Paris, on a site covering 1943 ha, one fifth of the area of Paris.

The Walt Disney Studios Park is based on the Disney Studios of Burbank, California, but features several exclusive new shows designed to catapult you right into the "action" of the cinema. Vaguely resembling a Mickey head on the map, this park is divided into four zones: Front Lot, Toon Studio, Hollywood Studio and Backlot. The attractions include a terrific white-knuckle ride, and there are several films and live shows that reveal some of the secrets behind cinema stunts and special effects. Two new rides were inaugurated for the 15th anniversary in 2007, and the Twilight Zone Tower of Terror brought further thrills in 2008. The Studios park is designed more for adolescents and adults than for small children, but there is still plenty of scope for future development.

sharing a dream

There's enough to keep you entertained from breakfast till bedtime, and if you want to enjoy your stay to the full, it's best to take it easy—don't try to cram everything into one day. Opening hours give you plenty of time to enjoy the attractions, and even when the lights have gone down on the parks, they continue to sparkle on Disney Village, a glitzy American-style boulevard full of restaurants, nightclubs, late-night shops, live concerts, everything imaginable to make sure you never get bored (and in full swing until 5 a.m.). As for accommodation, you have the choice of several huge resort hotels or, for those who come by car, the excellent camping facilities of Davy Crockett Ranch. For a change of pace, you can play tennis and golf, go swimming or skating (in winter), boating or jogging, or rise into the skies in a balloon. And every kind of service has been thought of, from animal care to pushchair rental.

Five minutes away from Marne-la-Vallée by RER train or shuttle bus from the resort hotels, the new town of Val d'Europe (Serris) is home to La Vallée® Outlet Shopping Village, where you can stock up on chic shopping bargains. Paris is just half an hour away by RER train. Excursions to other places of interest in the Ile-de-France region, such as the royal palace of Versailles, or the lovely medieval town of Provins, can be organized directly through the hotels or the tourist office.

FASTPASS

- Collect a Fastpass to save a long wait in the queues that quickly form at the most popular rides: Peter Pan's Flight, Big Thunder Mountain, Indiana Jones™ and the Temple of Peril, Star Tours, Space Mountain: Mission 2, Buzz Lightyear Laser Blast and the Twilight Zone Tower of Terror. Here's how to do it: at the entrance to the ride, insert your park entry ticket into the Fastpass distributor. It will deliver a ticket indicating a 60-minute time slot when you can come back and enter the attraction directly, by a separate entry gate. There's one restriction: you can only hold one Fastpass ticket at a time.

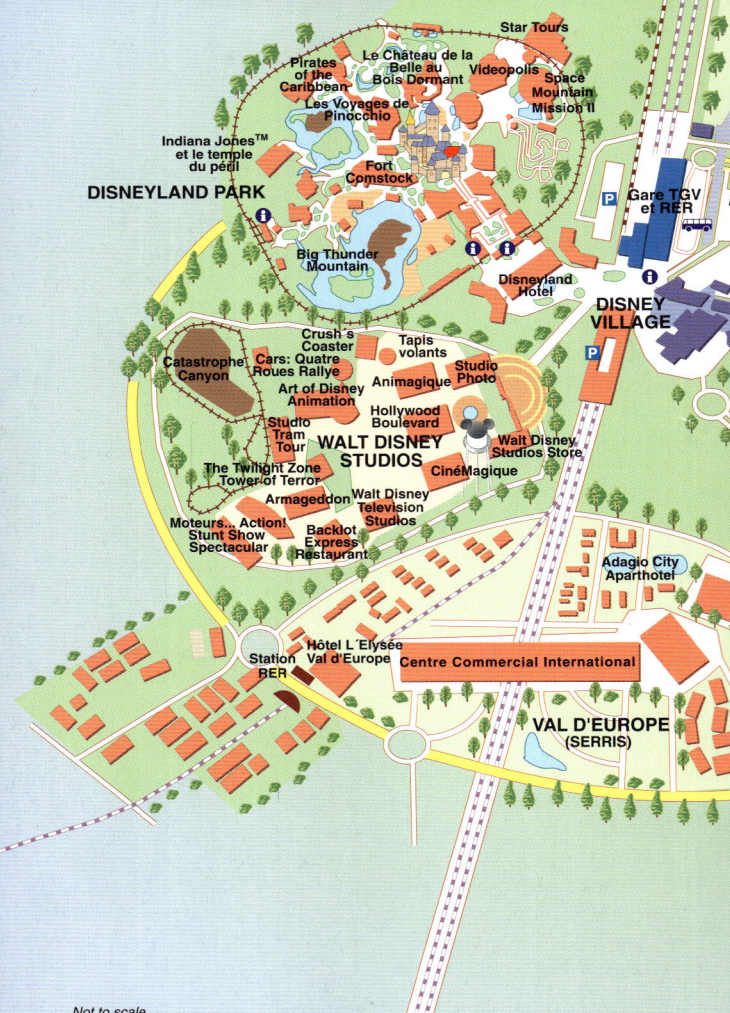

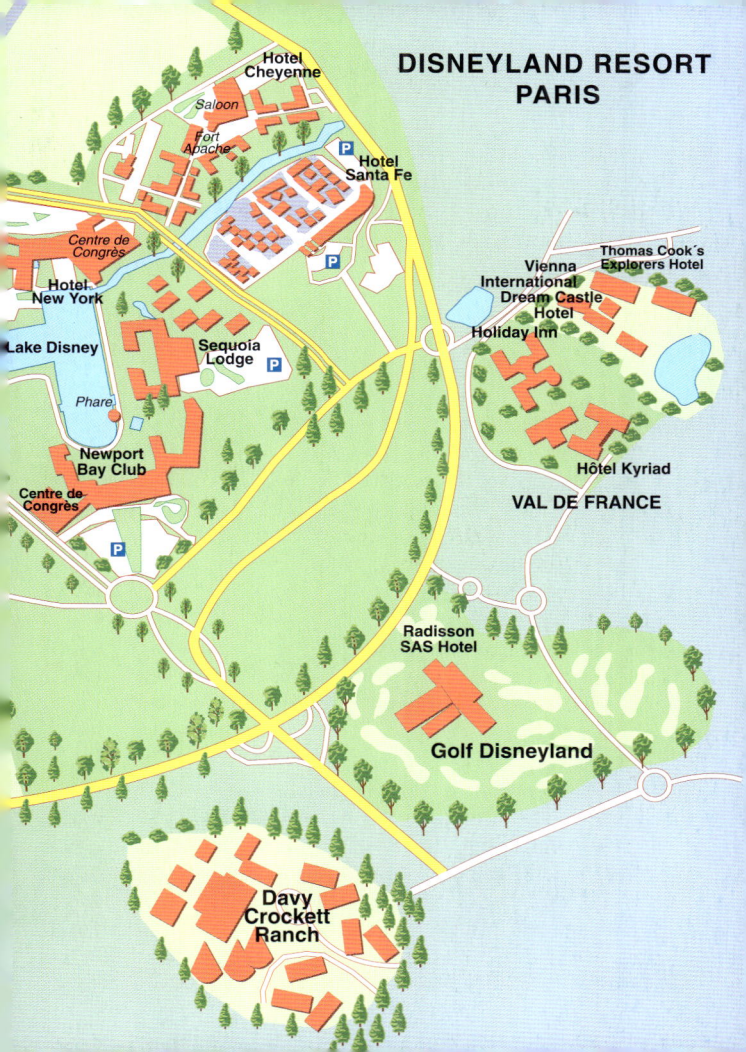

Once upon a time

Walter Elias Disney was born in Chicago, Illinois on December 5, 1901, son of Irish-Canadian Elias Disney, a building contractor, and Flora Call Disney, of German-American descent.

Early years
The family moved to a farm near Marceline, Missouri in 1906. Walt's skill at drawing was evident from an early age; he sold sketches to neighbours when only 7 years old. The Disneys moved to Kansas City where Walt took evening classes at the Academy of Fine Arts. In 1918, aged 16, he tried to enlist for military service but was turned down. He joined the Red Cross and was sent to France where he spent a year as ambulance driver and chauffeur to Red Cross officials, covering his ambulance with drawings and cartoons.

Walt Disney's first live action feature was the adventure movie Treasure Island, which was shot in England.

The first cartoons
Walt began work in a Kansas advertising studio in 1919, creating and marketing his first animated cartoons. In August 1923 he went to Hollywood with $40 in his pocket, to join his brother Roy. They borrowed money to set up the Disney Brothers Cartoon Studios, producing a series of short animated films, the *Alice Comedies*. In 1928 Walt created the character of Mickey Mouse (called Mortimer in early drafts) and lent him his own voice for *Steamboat Willie*, the first fully synchronized sound car-

toon. In 1932, *Flowers and Trees*, one of the *Silly Symphonies* cartoons, and the following year *The Three Little Pigs*, were both awarded Oscars. Donald Duck was created in 1934. The first animated film in colour, *The Band Concert*, appeared in 1935. Merchandising of Disney products began in 1935 with the characters featured on everything from biscuits to teapots. Manufactured by Ingersoll, 2 million Mickey Mouse wristwatches were sold in the first two months of issue.

Full-length films

Disney's first full-length film *Snow White and the Seven Dwarfs* (1937) was an immense success, and won another Oscar. *Pinocchio*, *Fantasia*, *Dumbo* and *Bambi* followed. By 1940 the Disney Studios employed over 1000 people.

World War II

Donald Duck starred in *Der Führer's Face*, an uncompromising satire of Nazi Germany which proved to be an effective morale-booster for the American troops on the battlefront. During the D-Day landings in Normandy, "Mickey Mouse" was used as a code name. In 1945, live action was combined for the first time with the cartoon medium in the musical *The Three Caballeros*.

The Fifties

Disney began television production in 1954, with *The Mickey Mouse Club* and *Zorro*, and continued to produce full-length cartoon films, including *Cinderella* (1850), *Alice in Wonderland* (1951), *Peter Pan* (1953), *Sleeping Beauty* (1959), as well as live-action films such as *20,000 Leagues Under the Sea* (1954) with James Mason and Kirk Douglas. In 1952 Walt Disney began to plan an amusement park where children and parents could have fun together; he bought 65 ha of orange groves in Anaheim, on the outskirts of Los Angeles. The project was financed by a television series, *Walt Disney's Disneyland*. Construction began in 1954 and one year later, on July 17, Disneyland was inaugurated.

The Sixties

Disney next turned his attentions to improving the quality of life in America. He bought 43 sq miles of land in Florida for Walt Disney World, an

Once upon a time

entire community of theme park, resort centre of hotels and motels, and the Experimental Prototype Community of Tomorrow — EPCOT. Walt Disney died on December 15, 1966, before completion of the project. Walt Disney World opened in 1971 and the Epcot Center in 1982.

Parks and more parks

Tokyo Disneyland opened in 1983, on land reclaimed from Tokyo Bay. At Walt Disney World in Florida, the Disney–MGM Studios Theme Park was inaugurated in 1989, paying homage to the magic of film-making as created by two of Hollywood's most famous studios. In 1987, an agreement was signed between the French authorities and The Walt Disney Company to build a theme park in Marne-la-Vallée, near Paris. A vast area of farmland, consisting mainly of sugar-beet fields, was purchased. Construction started in 1988 and Disneyland Paris was opened to the public on April 12, 1992. A railway station opened in 1994, permitting visitors from all over Europe to travel directly to the park entrance. New attractions were added continually over the decade, and finally the Walt Disney Studios Park was inaugurated on March 16, 2002 in the presence of Roy Disney, Walt's nephew.

Since spring, 2003, five new "Disney-recommended" hotels have opened, four in nearby Val de France and one on the golf course, complete with wellness & fitness centre.

FRENCH CONNECTION

It's quite possible that Walt Disney had French ancestors. Way back in 1066, when the Normans defeated King Harold at the Battle of Hastings, two French soldiers, Hughes and his son Robert d'Isigny, from the village of Isigny-sur-Mer in Normandy, decided to stay in England. Over the centuries, the name changed to Disney. A branch of the family moved to Ireland in the 17th century, and their descendants Arundel Elias and his brother Robert Disney emigrated to America in 1834. Nowadays Isigny-sur-Mer is particularly known for its Camembert cheese.

Disneyland Park

Walt Disney loved model trains, and in 1947 he laid out miniature tracks all round his home, tunneling under his wife's rose garden.

When he launched his own theme park in Anaheim in the 1950s, he designed it in the same way, with an almost lifesize railway outlining the perimeter of five "lands", and the main station at the entrance to Main Street, U.S.A. The Disneyland Park in Paris follows the same plan.

Once through the main entrance gates, you pass beneath the railroad station to find yourself in **Town Square**, with an old-fashioned bandstand in the middle. Straight ahead, Main Street leads directly to **Central Plaza**, beneath the blue and gold turrets of Sleeping Beauty's Castle (here given its French name, Le Château de la Belle au Bois Dormant). The paths to the other "lands" fan out from Central Plaza.

For the sake of convenience, our guide visits each land in a clockwise direction, but of course you can organize your visit any way you please. Small children will particularly appreciate Fantasyland, older ones Frontierland and Adventureland, adolescents prefer Discoveryland. Grown-ups love everything.

IN THE KNOW

At the park entrance, pick up the two leaflets, *Park Guide* and *Programme*. The little guide includes a handy map, lists which attractions are open and provides information on restaurant bookings and practical hints. The *Programme*, printed in several languages, gives more precise details of parade times, where to meet the Disney characters, and how to book tickets for special shows. If you miss these at the entrance, call in at City Hall. Other information, such as filming locations and waiting times, is posted on the noticeboard at Central Plaza.

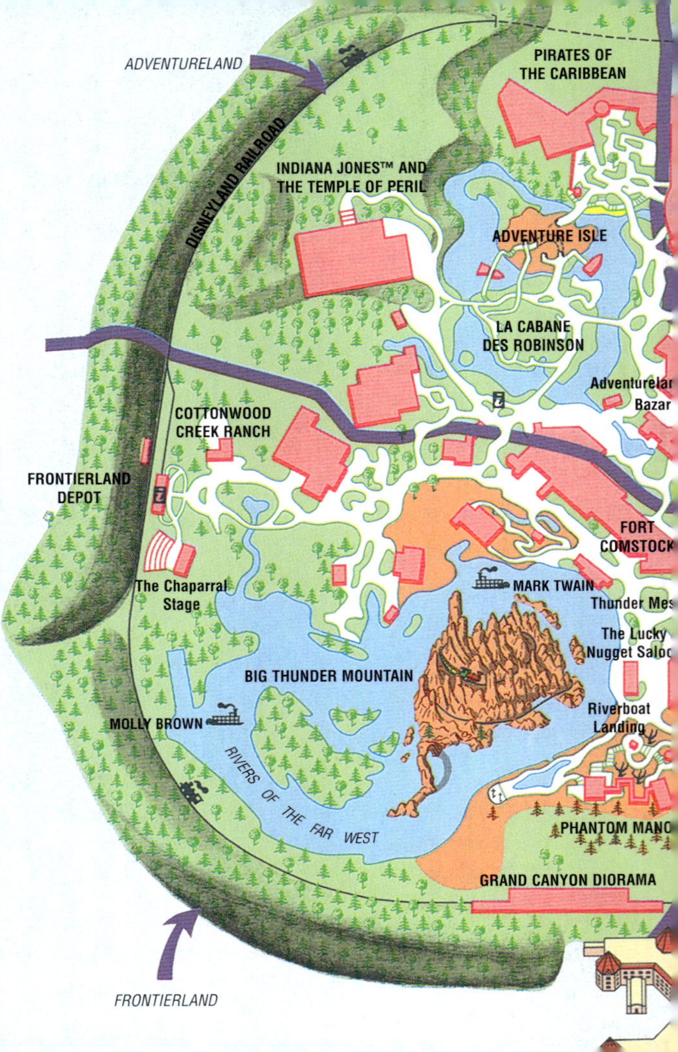

ADVENTURELAND

PIRATES OF THE CARIBBEAN

INDIANA JONES™ AND THE TEMPLE OF PERIL

ADVENTURE ISLE

LA CABANE DES ROBINSON

Adventureland Bazar

COTTONWOOD CREEK RANCH

FRONTIERLAND DEPOT

FORT COMSTOCK

The Chaparral Stage

MARK TWAIN

Thunder Mesa

The Lucky Nugget Saloon

BIG THUNDER MOUNTAIN

Riverboat Landing

MOLLY BROWN

RIVERS OF THE FAR WEST

PHANTOM MANOR

GRAND CANYON DIORAMA

DISNEYLAND RAILROAD

© MICHELIN

FRONTIERLAND

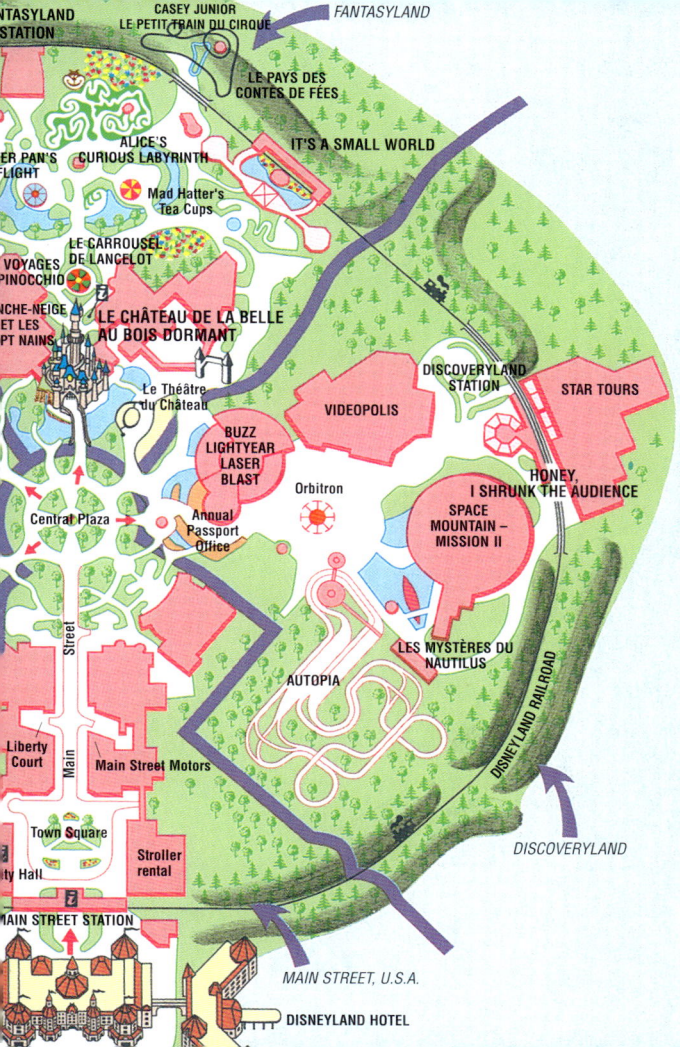

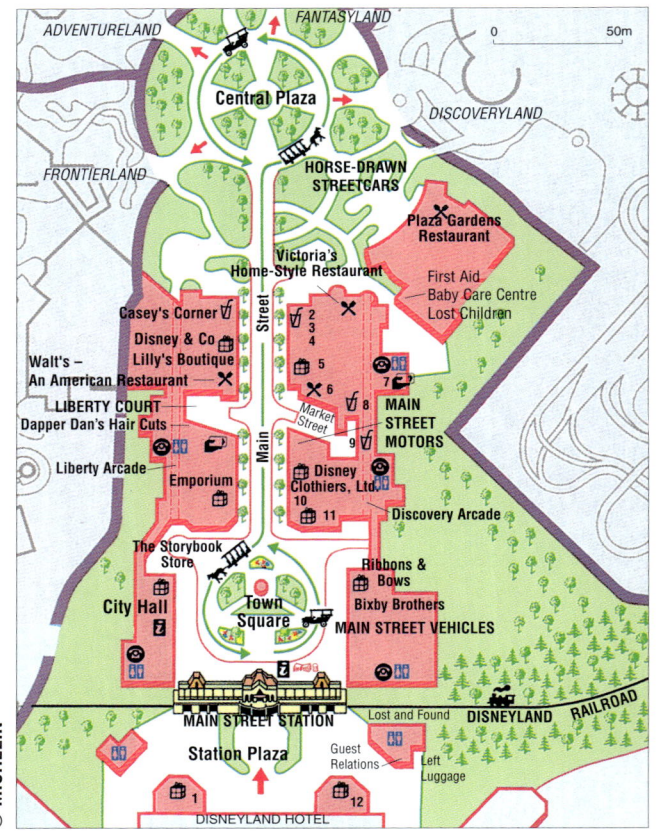

Main Street U.S.A. *1 Plaza West Boutique; 2 The Gibson Girl Ice Cream Parlour; 3 Cookie Kitchen; 4 Cable Car Bake Shop; 5 Harrington's Fine China and Porcelains, Disneyana Collectibles, Glass Fantasies; 6 Market House Deli; 7 Cash distributors; 8 The Coffee Grinder; 9 The Ice Cream Company; 10 Boardwalk Candy Palace; 11 Town Square Photography; 12 Plaza East Boutique.*

■ Main Street U.S.A.

Not just any old main street, this is a charming, turn-of-the-century boulevard based on Walt Disney's childhood hometown, Marceline, Missouri. **Streetcars** drawn by powerful Percheron horses rumble past the pretty, pastel-painted façades, while vintage fire engines and paddy wagons ferry visitors from Town Square to Central Plaza. You'll hear the whistle and chuff of a steam engine as you pass beneath the arches of Main Street Station – but save your train ride for later in the day, when the queues are shorter (after the big parade, for instance).

Most of the services are grouped in this part of the park, and both sides of the street are lined with shops, restaurants and cafés (described in detail in later chapters of this guide). To the right, just beyond the entrance, is the pick-up point for pushchairs (strollers) or wheelchairs. Opposite, **City Hall** is a key meeting point and the best place to pick up information or make hotel bookings.

At Christmas, a huge tree is set up at Town Square, and all Main Street is illuminated with fairy lights. In the evening, everyone gathers here for a charming ceremony, when a child from the crowd is chosen to wave a magic wand and light up the tree.

Covered arcades along each side of the street provide sheltered access to all the shops and restaurants. In each one there are telephones, cloakrooms and cash distributors. On the west side, the wonderfully ornate **Liberty Arcade** displays plans and photos tracing the construction of the Statue of Liberty and its restoration. The

AUTOGRAPHS

Always have a pen and autograph book (and a camera) at the ready. If you arrive when the park opens, you'll encounter a host of cheery Disney characters ready to sign their names and pose for photos around Town Square. As for Mickey Mouse, you'll find him with his minder in a specially cordoned-off area near Casey's Corner, where he spends all morning hugging and signing autographs for all the children who wait patiently in line.

Disneyland Park

Statue of Liberty Tableau commemorates the inauguration of the famous lady, October 28, 1886.

About half-way along this side, tucked away in the corner of Liberty Court, **Dapper Dan's Hair Cuts** is an old-fashioned barbershop resplendent with mahogany panelling. Real men come here for the closest shave of their life, with brush, soap and strophoned cut-throat razor. They are awarded a diploma testifying to their bravery.

Discovery Arcade on the east side of Main Street is dedicated to the spirit of invention, its showcases full of scale models, sketches and blueprints for cities of the future. At its northern end you'll find a First Aid and Baby Care Centre, and the meeting place for lost children.

Disneyland Railroad

The trains from Main Street Station circle the park in 20 minutes, running every seven minutes or so. You can get off or board the train at any of the other stations along the way. It's a scenic and restful way of getting from one "land" to another. Almost as soon as the train chugs out of Main Street Station, it disappears into the **Grand Canyon Diorama**, an attraction that can only be seen from the train (on the right-hand side). As you progress from scene to scene, the light changes from dawn to dusk; the air fills with the animal howls and bird calls.

Continuing its tour, the train puffs past a landscape of gushing geysers, with Frontierland's spectacular **Big Thunder Mountain** as a backdrop, and on to Adventureland, where you may catch sight of the abandoned base camp of Indiana Jones. Soon you plunge into the gloomy caverns of the **Pirates of the Caribbean**, with glimpses of the moon-lit Blue Lagoon Restaurant. Next comes Fantasyland, and finally the futuristic visions of Discoveryland, before the terminus at Main Street Station.

Parades

Morning, afternoon and evening, colourful parades, with plenty of ear-blasting music, lively dancing and simply stunning costumes, make a break between rides. The floats start out in Fantasyland, to the right of It's a Small World, skirt the castle, circle Central Plaza then roll along Main Street, U.S.A., ending at Town Square. The theme changes throughout the

Main Street U.S.A.

year—Carnival, Halloween, Christmas, and so on, and feature characters from the latest Disney releases along with timeless favourites. See the *Programme* for the exact times (and if you've already seen the parade, this is a great opportunity to visit Space Mountain in peace!). Excited spectators start bagging the best spots along the parade route at least half an hour before the fun is due to start. The least-crowded viewing areas are in Fantasyland, in front of Fizzeria Bella Notte and It's a Small World. Special areas are reserved for people in wheelchairs on Central Plaza, opposite the castle, in Fantasyland next to It's a Small World, and at Town Square in front of Ribbons and Bows Hat Shop.

Frontierland

Frontierland

The stampede out West was mostly triggered by the desire for gold, and Frontierland is fittingly built around the idea of a mining community complete with trading stores and saloon.

To reach the rustic little town of Thunder Mesa, leave Central Plaza in the direction of Fort Comstock, and step right into **Legends of the Wild West**, a pioneer outpost comprising cavalry quarters, jail and Indian tepee village.

Big Thunder Mountain

At the heart of town, the Big Thunder Mining Company runs the rickety mine trains that rattle round Big Thunder Mountain, a red, rugged pile of wind-lashed sandstone pinnacles, mesa plateaux, canyons and natural bridges looking for all the world like a setting for your favourite western. Board a train at the loading platform in the mainland office of the mining company. Surging up and clattering down, swerving round bends, through tunnels of stalactites and a cave of bats, the train offers some of the best thrills in the whole of Disneyland Park – not to be missed!

Phantom Manor

Ready for something scary? How about paying a visit to Phantom Manor? This eerie old mansion, perched on a hill, was the home of one of Thunder Mesa's founding families. The daughter of the house was jilted on her wedding day and never seen again – or rather, never seen *alive* again. Dare you go in?

Venture through the manor gates past the Riverboat Landing. Even the trees look as though they are in mourning. As you wait at the Garden Pavilion, you'll sense something in the air – a whisper in the wind, the distant sound of voices and laughter, the tinkle of crystal, the far-off strains of music, a whining shutter. The house beckons, but beware! Once through the doors, they will creak shut behind you and you're trapped. A traumatic descent in an elevator, a race down a gloomy corridor, and you board a lugubrious "doom buggy" to glide through cobwebbed halls, peopled by more ghosts, ghouls and spectres than you'd care to imagine. Countless hair-raising surprises lie in store before you stagger outside.

Gather your wits together in **Boot Hill** graveyard on the river bank

Disneyland Park

beside the mansion. It's full of high-spirited fun, with jokey epitaphs engraved on the tombstones.

Rivers of the Far West

At the Riverboat Landing, board one of the paddle wheelers *Molly Brown* or *Mark Twain* for a trip around the Rivers of the Far West. From the upper deck, you'll watch a superb panorama unfold as you glide past Big Thunder Mountain and Wilderness Island, the peace suddenly shattered as a mine train hurtles out of nowhere amid the delighted squeals of its passengers.

Down by the water's edge, **Pocahontas Indian Village** is a playground where your little ones can run around and let off some steam. Go down to the edge of the water for a great view of Big Thunder Mountain.

Rustler Roundup Shootin' Gallery

Try your hand at bringing a bunch of dangerous outlaws to justice at the shooting gallery, near the mining company's office. You'll have to put a €2 coin in the slot for the privilege – but think of the good you'll be doing society!

A train rattles down the slopes of Big Thunder Mountain

Critter Corral

During the summer season, children can stroke (but not feed) the cute little animals at Critter Corral, an atmospheric old farm near the Cottonwood Creek Ranch. (Closes at dusk.)

Chaparral Stage

Mickey, Minnie and friends present hilarious shows in this large, covered wooden theatre, several times a day. See the *Programme* for times.

Adventureland

Inspired by the heroes and villains of childhood tales — *The Arabian Nights, Treasure Island, Swiss Family Robinson* — Adventureland is the haunt of pirates, explorers and castaways.

The gateway to Adventureland leads straight into an Arabian bazaar, an exotic desert city of ochre sandstone, with painted onion domes, overhanging wooden balconies and tiny courtyards.

Le Passage Enchanté d'Aladdin

A fascinating walk-through attraction, past colourful scenes of the Walt Disney film, *Aladdin*.

Indiana Jones™ *FASTPASS* and the Temple of Péril

This roller-coaster with a difference plunges you deep into the heart of the jungle, on the tracks of the intrepid archaeologist Indy among the ruins of the Lost City. The first 360° loop in Disney history!

Adventure Isle

Cross over to the island by one of the bridges: rickety planks balancing on barrels, a suspension bridge swaying over a waterfall — or a sturdier, more traditional bridge for those not quite able to face such perils. Tunnels burrow deep into the rock at every turn, providing the ideal place for a secret treasure trove and hidden pirates' lairs. Coves and caves honeycomb the land where bloody disputes between rogues once took place and many a villain lay low.

The Swiss Family Robinson were shipwrecked just offshore, while fleeing the hardships of the Napoleonic Wars, and built their tree-house in the south of the island. Feel free to study their life-style at leisure in **La Cabane des Robinson**, high in the branches of a banyan tree. Climb the spiral staircase to reach it — the family is not likely to be at home but you can sneak a look at the view through their telescope and look around the house. On the first floor are the kitchen and library, above them the living room, fitted out in bamboo, and higher still, the bedrooms, constructed from beams saved from the wreckage of the good ship *The Swallow* (which you can also visit in the creek). Food is stored in the cellar in a network of caves down in the tree's roots (Le

Adventureland

A L'Epave; B Skull Rock; C Ben Gunn's Cave; D Pirate Lookout

Adventureland

Ventre de la Terre). Note the ingenious system of rope pulley and water wheel bringing fresh water to the kitchen sink in bamboo cups and pipes.

On the north side of the island is **Ben Gunn's Cave**, where Jim Hawkins and Long John Silver of Treasure Island fought for the hidden booty. Six paths lead into the underground hideaway, between **Skull Rock** and **Spyglass Hill**.

Young buccaneers (from 3 to 9 years) are welcome to walk the plank at **Pirates' Beach**, an adventure playground complete with sand and wrecked boat.

Pirates of the Caribbean

In a massive grey stone fortress at the far end of Adventureland, this is one of the most popular and exciting of all the attractions of Disneyland Park. You'll drift slowly through the pirates' haunt, watching one swashbuckling scene after another, performed by an astounding cast of 124 Audio-Animatronics® figures, the "almost human" characters invented by the Walt Disney Imagineers. The ribald, rousing scenes, the individualized characters of the buccaneers, as well as the sheer technical mastery of their speech, songs and facial expressions, are truly amazing.

Fantasyland

1 La Boutique du Château; 2 La Confiserie des Trois Fées

Fantasyland

Cross the drawbridge from Central Plaza into Fantasyland, where fairy tales have come to life with a wave of Walt Disney's magic wand.

Le Château de la Belle au Bois Dormant

Symbol and centrepiece of the whole park, the pink castle with its blue and gold roof-tiles is technically an astonishing achievement, looking much taller than its actual 45 m (147 ft) thanks to a cinematic technique used for its construction known as forced perspective – the bricks used for the lower rows are cut much bigger than those at the top. No fewer than 14 layers of paint were needed to obtain the right shade of pink. It's the epitome of fairy-tale castles, drawing influences from ancient tapestries, illustrations from the medieval manuscripts of *Les Très Riches Heures du Duc de Berry*, and the Disney animated film, *Sleeping Beauty*.

Once inside, turn round and look up at the magic oval window to see it change. A spiral staircase leads to **La Galerie de la Belle au Bois Dormant**, where the tale of Sleeping Beauty is related in illuminated manuscripts, stained-glass windows and handwoven Aubusson tapestries.

Down the stairs, in **La Tanière du Dragon**, a greasy grey monster lies rumbling in its cave, waking up now and then to hiss and snort a cloud of smoke, blinking a nasty red eye.

Excalibur

In the courtyard of the castle, King Arthur's sword is held fast in a stone. Certain children (probably those who eat all their vegetables) have been seen to glide it out with next to no effort at all, and received a certificate to prove it from Merlin himself.

Blanche-Neige et les Sept Nains

A forbidding grey building by the castle is the home of the Wicked Queen, spying from an upper balcony. The trip around this dark ride starts in her dungeon, where she is mixing up her poison to get rid of Snow White. You'll get to see the Seven Dwarfs in their cottage, their diamond mine, and the queen's castle with her magic mirror on the wall. All ends well, of course, with Snow White and Prince Charming going off to their castle to live happily ever after.

Disneyland Park

Les Voyages de Pinocchio
Ride through the adventures of Pinocchio comfortably seated in a hand-crafted cart, setting out from the little Italian village where the toy maker Geppetto sculpted the wooden puppet, on to Pleasure Island and finally back to the toy shop where the Blue Fairy turns Pinocchio into a real boy.

Le Carrousel de Lancelot
Outside now, for a ride on this enormous merry-go-round, perhaps the biggest in Europe with 86 elegant horses prancing and galloping in a whirlwind of colour and music.

Dumbo the Flying Elephant
Yes, elephants can fly, and here you can climb on Dumbo's back and soar as high or as low as you like – the commands are in your hands.

Mad Hatter's Tea Cups
Back on ground level, settle yourself down inside a tea cup for a wild spin among the crockery at the Mad Hatter's tea party. There's a steering wheel so you can decide for yourself how fast and in which direction you want to turn.

Peter Pan's Flight
Take the covered wooden bridge from Pinocchio's village to the home of the Darling family and join Peter Pan and Wendy. You board a pirate galleon to fly through the clouds over the roofs of London to Never Never Land, where Captain Hook, the greedy crocodile, Tinker Bell and all the other familiar characters from J.M. Barrie's story relive their adventures. This is the most popular ride in the whole park – pick up a Fastpass.

Alice's Curious Labyrinth
Now you can get nicely lost in this intriguing maze of yew hedges, also based on *Alice in Wonderland*, where you'll meet familiar characters at every twist and turn. Misleading signs point out "This Way", "Which Way", "Go Back" – and don't count on any advice from the Cheshire Cat. Look out for those funny drops of water, leaping along the top of a hedge. Then tackle the next part of the labyrinth, full of frustrating dead ends, till you reach the knobbly purple castle of the Queen of Hearts.

After all that, you'll be thankful for a rest at **March Hare Refreshments**, the perfect place to untangle your

Fantasyland

brain and enjoy a piece of Alice's "unbirthday" cake.

Les Pirouettes du Vieux Moulin
Take a ride in a wooden bucket to the top of this Ferris wheel for a panoramic view over the park.

It's a Small World
This is Disneyland's musical tribute to the children of the earth, justifiably claimed to be the happiest cruise that ever sailed round the world. Board a flat-bottomed boat and drift slowly past London, Venice, Moscow, the Far East, through all the continents, a marvellous voyage with 281 costumed dolls and toys bringing all countries and races together on the theme of the unity of mankind. The show was first presented in New York at the World's Fair, in aid of UNICEF.

Le Pays des Contes de Fées
Aboard a small canal boat, you will glide through a fantasy world of miniature villages and landscapes, each featuring characters from favourite fairy tales.

To see the same scenes from another perspective, hop aboard **Casey Jr. le Petit Train du Cirque**, a joyous string of brightly coloured carriages inspired by the circus train featured in the film *Dumbo*.

Discoveryland

Discoveryland

With flashing lights and laser beams, Discoveryland looks into the worlds of yesterday, today and tomorrow.

Space Mountain – Mission II

Imagine how it feels to be catapulted into the dark depths of outer space by a cannon, shooting past the stars, almost colliding with meteorites, turning upside down, looping, corkscrewing – and all over again!

Inspired by the machine invented by Jules Verne in *From the Earth to the Moon*, Space Mountain is a miracle of modern technology. But it's not for the faint-hearted. Take the advice of a survivor: keep your head firmly on the headrest all through the trip.

More special effects and sensational features were added in 2005, making this one of the most popular rides in the park. The queues can be long, so it's worth getting a Fastpass. For safety reasons, a minimum height of 1 m 40 (4 ft 7 in), is required. If you feel a bit queasy about embarking on this adventure, see it from the safety of the observation platform that reveals all the inner workings.

Afterwards, recover your senses by exploring **Les Mystères du Nautilus**, the workrooms and living quarters of

Disneyland Park

Captain Nemo, Jules Verne's sinister character whose fantastic submarine is berthed in the lagoon. Watch out for the giant octopus!

Honey, I Shrunk the Audience

Lose all sense of reality as you settle down to watch the crazy experiments of Professor Wayne Szalinski, inventor of the famous machine that shrinks anything coming under its beam. Make sure you wear your safety goggles, and keep your feet firmly on the ground. One catastrophe follows another as the professor's children take control of the machine. Hey, watch out – it's pointing at you…

Buzz Lightyear Laser Blast

Inspired by the film Toy Story 2, this attraction opened in April 2006. Buzz Lightyear and the world of toys need your help – Emperor Zurg and his team of little green Martians are stealing their batteries!

All recruited Space Rangers board a revolving shuttle for an intergalactic adventure: armed with laser pistols you have to combat the enemy on moving targets. Points are scored on individual screens. Buzz Lightyear himself visits the attraction several times a day and poses for photographs with his heroic Space Ranger warriors.

Discoveryland

Star Tours

A fascinating flight-simulator similar to those used to train pilots. Tuck your bags under the seat, fasten your seat belt, and off you set on a hair-raising intergalactic trip.

Be sure to stop off at **L'Astroport Services Interstellaires** to try out the last word in computer games.

Videopolis

Fabulous live shows, dance and music videos are presented at Videopolis, where lasers and special effects create a first-class show. See the *Programme* for times of performances.

Arcade Alpha and **Arcade Beta** on either side of the main entrance are packed with video games.

Orbitron

Sketches by Leonardo da Vinci inspired the design of this merry-go-round with a difference. Hop into a spaceship and pilot it through the cosmos.

Autopia

Driving is a pleasure in Autopia, where children and parents alike love to negotiate the twists and hairpin bends of this futuristic race track.

DID YOU KNOW

The names painted on the windows of the upper storeys of Main Street are credits to those who contributed towards the creation of Disneyland.

The 16 outside horses of the Carrousel de Lancelot are painted with 23-carat gold leaf

More than 70 gardeners tend the 12,000 trees, 141,000 bushes, 20,000 sq m of lawns and thousands of flowers.

Count the colours in It's A Small World: 150 different shades in all!

All the props you see in Big Thunder Mountain are genuine antiques.

Disney Village, with its aluminium columns, was originally designed by Frank Gehry, though his concept has been modified through the years.

Walt Disney Studios Park

Like Alice passing through the Looking Glass, when you enter the Walt Disney Studios Park you find yourself on the other side of the silver screen.

Don't forget to pick up a *Programme* for show and parade times, and indications on where to meet your favourite Disney characters.

■ Front Lot

Through the main gates is a pretty courtyard, Place des Frères Lumière, in neo-Hispanic style, refreshed by a fountain depicting Mickey in his Sorcerer's Apprentice costume. Above it looms the symbol of the park, a 33-m tall reservoir sporting the inevitable Mickey Mouse ears – dwarfed now by the yellow skyscrapers of the Tower of Terror.

All the park services are grouped on the right-hand side of the courtyard in buildings representing the offices of a real studio. There's a *bureau de change*; an information centre, **Studio Services**; the pick-up point for pushchairs and wheelchairs; a first-aid centre; a meeting place for lost children; toilets and **Studio Photo**, a film and camera shop. Opposite is **Walt Disney Studios Store**.

Enter **Studio 1** and plunge straight into the atmosphere of Hollywood in the flirty Thirties. Frantic activity, posters and clapboards will soon convince you that you are a star yourself, part of the film *Lights, Camera, Action!* You're allowed to twiddle with the the lighting or fiddle with the special effects. This is **Hollywood Boulevard**, where a series of façades conceal a restaurant on one side, and a store on the other. They depict real and imaginary buildings – *Schwab's Pharmacy*, for example, was a well-known drugstore and meeting place of actors and writers in the 1940s, and the *Brown Derby*, shaped like a bowler hat, was a favourite restaurant of the Hollywood stars. A peek behind the scenes will reveal that these are just façades, constructed in exactly the same way as real stage sets.

Walt Disney Studios Park

■ Toon Studio

Turn right when you come out of Studio 1 and enter a dazzling realm of blue and gold, set against the colourful backdrop of ToonTown. Formerly Animation Courtyard, this part of the park is dedicated to the art of animated film, exploring every aspect of trick photography, comic strips and optical illusions.

Animagique

Settle down in your armchair: the lights dim and the curtain rises on Micky Mouse and Donald Duck, both larger than life, trying their hand at illustration. Donald, of course, can't help but get into mischief, and opens up the film archives, letting loose all your favourite characters from Disney films – the pink elephants from *Dumbo*, King Louie and friends from *Jungle Book*, Simba and Rafiki from *The Lion King*, Pinocchio and Jiminy Cricket. They come to life and cause a merry havoc in this extraordinary show created specially for the Walt Disney Studios Park. The action is skilfully manipulated in a technique combining Japanese *bunraku*, and

Toon Studio

the Black Light theatre of Prague. The effect is utterly enchanting – don't miss the fluttery butterflies and the gorgeous dancing jellyfish!

Flying Carpets over Agrabah

Fly away into the sunset over the town of Agrabah in this colourful merry-go-round, a whirlwind of magic carpets spirited up by the genial Genie from his magic lamp. Drivers in the front seats can control the height of their enchanted vehicle; back-seat passengers can make it ripple up and down.

Crush's Coaster

Discover the thrilling underwater world of Nemo and other friends from the Pixar film, *Finding Nemo*, on this new dark ride and rollercoaster! Setting off from Sydney pier, you will board a spinning turtle, twist and turn through a coral reef, plunge down a waterfall, float alongside the clownfish Nemo and a shoal of his friends, then explore a sunken submarine. Keep your eyes peeled: could that be a shark lurking in those shadows? or two – or three? Just pray your turtle will get you safely back to shore!

Cars: Quatre Roues Rallye

Based on another great Pixar comedy, *Cars*, this mind-bending new merry-go-round transports you to the town of Radiator Springs, somewhere in the American desert, against the stunning backdrop of the Grand Canyon rock formations. See if you can keep your vehicle under control as it hurtles along the racetrack of the Piston Cup, spiralling through a figure of eight from one level to another, and spinning round and round.

Art of Disney Animation

Beneath the big pointed hat of the sorcerer's apprentice, this "hands-on" attraction begins by sending you back tens of thousands of years, to the times when our prehistoric ancestors improved the interior decoration of their caves by painting wall pictures of animals. Fast forward throughout the years and you will discover a Greek urn painted like a comic strip, a shadow-puppet from Java, and a series of weird and wonderful inventions like the zoetrope, the phenakistoscope, a thaumatrope, and a praxinoscope. You can work them all yourself, and no, the mutoscope will not turn you into a mutant.

Walt Disney Studios Park

Before the doors to the main show open, you can also look around at drawings from the first Disney animated films, *Alice Comedies* and *Snow White and the Seven Dwarfs*, while Walt Disney himself outlines on video the history of animated cartoons.

The next stage of the show, in the Disney Classics Theater, is a nostalgic 8-minute film resuming the best moments of the Disney cartoons. You then move into another room, Drawn to Animation, where an animator at his drawing desk explains how the characters are created and how life is breathed into them, with the help of Mushu, the feisty little dragon from *Mulan*.

Finally, you discover a studio with several "animation stations" where you can sit down and learn how to draw Donald Duck and other characters yourself—and keep your works of art to take home. You can also design a scenario for a zoetrope, try out your skills at dubbing or making sound effects, colour in characters and see how they fit into the background, and learn how to change their expressions and make them move.

Hollywood Studio

■ **Hollywood Studio**

Turning left from Studio 1, you get to experience life behind the scenes of movie and television production. See how the cameras work, how stage sets are made, costumes designed and special effects invented. And it all ends in total catastrophe!

CinéMagique

Do not miss this fantastic movie where it becomes impossible to draw the line between imagination and reality. Incorporating clips from over 60 great films tracing the history of the cinema from its very beginnings, it will revive nostalgic memories as scenes from old comedies and westerns pass over the huge screen. Before it all starts, admire the Art deco design of the splendid movie theatre, and most important: don't forget to switch off your mobile phone! And make sure you have some tissues handy: the unlikely hero will be forced to make a heartbreaking decision between love in a dream world and loneliness in real life.

Full of amazing special effects, the exclusive scenario for the Walt Disney Studios Park features French film star Julie Delpy as the heroine, Tchéky Karyo as the knight in shining armour, Scottish actor Alan Cumming as the wizard and Canadian comedian Martin Short in the role of the irresistible hero.

STREET THEATRE

- Groups of musicians, masters of improvisation, gaggles of Disney characters, Goofy and Pluto, Chip and Dale, the hairy guys from Monsters, Inc., – all around the park you'll come across these genial entertainers who'll keep you laughing between rides and attractions. Mickey and Minnie, Donald Duck, Daisy and Scrooge McDuck are always happy to pose for a souvenir photo or sign an autograph.

Walt Disney Television Studios

The big building labelled Studio 4 originally housed the working studios for Disney Channel France, part of a European cable network. These have now moved elsewhere, and the space is now used for a new attraction: **Stitch Live!** Visitors can "converse"

39

Walt Disney Studios Park

with the big-eared bundle of blue fur that is Stitch, the alien puppy.

Afterwards, head for **Disney Channel Cyber Space** where you can design your own rollercoaster, then try it out in the **CyberSpace Mountain** and see how you score for scariness. There's also a fantastic array of video games and simulators to try out.

The Twilight Zone Tower of Terror

The scene is set. Imagine the Hollywood Tower Hotel, an Art Deco gem in sandy yellow, soaring over the California hills. During Halloween in 1939, ten years after the hotel's inauguration, guests flocked to a party in the ballroom of the 13th floor. But lightning struck – and the elevator with its 5 passengers was transported into the "twilight zone" at the very same moment that part of the hotel was destroyed. Its ruins remain, a great crack splitting the side of the tower from top to bottom.

Your visit begins with a look around the hotel library, where a short film gives an outline of the tragic events. You then walk through the service areas to the boiler room, and board the elevator waiting to waft you up to the fatal 13th floor... As you rise, the doors open, you catch a glimpse of a corridor peopled by beckoning spirits. Sit fast, you are about to enter the twilight zone yourself! Woooh, a free fall faster than gravity will send your senses reeling!

Studio Tram Tour

Hop aboard a tram and trundle staidly through the areas of a cinema studio that are normally hidden from view. The trip (commented on video screen) reveals stage sets and prop storage areas, accessories, costumes and special effects from famous

Hollywood Studio

movies. You'll see pterodactyls and the gateway to Waterfall City from the new American TV mini series *Dinotopia*, planes from *Pearl Harbor*, and a collection of famous vehicles including Cruella de Vil's vintage black-spotted car from *102 Dalmatians* and *Herbie, the Lovebug*.

You'll soon find out what it means to be in the hot seat as your tram makes a detour through **Catastrophe Canyon**, an outdoor set designed for large-scale special effects. The earthquake isn't too bad, and you probably won't even get singed in the conflagration, but there's a dam about to burst… keep cool!

Survivors go behind the scenes to see the impressive mechanisms that caused all the uproar.

Back on the road, you will travel through between sets from the film *Reign of Fire*, through the streets of London devastated by fire-breathing dragons. Watch out, it looks as though they are still on the rampage!

Panic strikes aboard the tram as a tanker full of petrol suddenly begins to slide down the side of the canyon!

Walt Disney Studios Park

■ Backlot

If it's action you're looking for, head straight for Backlot, where a bone-rattling encounter with a meteorite, a mind-bending stunt show and an ear-splitting rollercoaster provide tons of thrills and spills. Count yourself lucky if you get home in one piece.

Armageddon Special Effects

Armadillo, a space ship from the film *Armageddon*, stands outside this attraction, which will help you understand the science of cinematographic special effects, first invented by the illusionist Georges Méliès and used in his film *Voyage to the Moon* (1902). You'll see how techniques evolved in the past hundred years, to the state-of-the-art technology used in the movies today.

After a little spiel from a host expert in special effects, some audience participation and a short demonstration of pyrotechnic explosions, you climb aboard a replica of the Russian space station Mir and set off for the stars. Needless to say, nothing goes according to plan… Smoke, sparks, metal creaks, a wall cracks, suddenly a giant fireball explodes through the central shaft! Hold on tight!

Rock'n'Roller Coaster starring Aerosmith

Walk through the rock group's recording studios, strap yourself into a Soundtracker and zoom like lightning into the fastest ride ever created for a Disney theme park. After the countdown, you accelerate from zero to 100 km/h in 2.8 seconds, riding through twists, turns, loops and corkscrew, upside down and rightside up, while the terrific sound, speed and light blast you right into the beat of the music.

If you can manage to listen to the words, you may notice that the lyrics have been changed: the classic *Love in an Elevator* was re-recorded as *Love in a Roller Coaster*, while *What Kind of Love are You On?* becomes *What Kind of Ride are You On?*

Ready for another go?

Stunt Show Spectacular

Rémy Julienne, the most famous of all French dare-devil stuntsmen, has worked together with the Disney Imagineers to devise this fabulous show, performed several times a day to an audience of up to 3,000 (get there 30 minutes before the start to be sure of a good seat). The scene is a pretty

Backlot

market square in a Mediterranean village, the stunts involve specially designed cars, motorbikes and a jetski, a hero, several baddies in hot pursuit, and members of the audience acting as extras. Repeats of the action are shown on a giant screen, with slow-motion views and sound effects — and plenty of surprises in store. On the way out, you may be lucky enough to meet the stuntmen who'll be pleased to sign your autograph book.

Disney Village

With its flashing neon and throbbing music, Disney Village is a sort of transition zone between the parks and the hotels. Its shops stay open until midnight (1 a.m. on Fridays and Saturdays), and some of the restaurants even later (see also pp. 48–49 and 54–55).

Concerts, festivals, parties and all kinds of fun are organized at the Central Stage and in the clubs. Shows and musicals are hosted in the white tent-like **Dôme**, behind McDonalds. For programmes, see the Event calendar on www.disneylandparis.com

Revellers might check out the club music (from 11 p.m.) at **Hurricane's** discotheque, or dance to the foot-tapping tempo of the live cowboy band at **Billy Bob's Country Western Saloon** (from 6 p.m. weekdays, from 7 p.m. at weekends).

The menfolk just adore the **Sports Bar**, where they can watch the latest match over a beer. Most major events are broadcast (from 6 p.m. weekdays, from noon at weekends).

Opposite the Sports Bar, the **Nex Game Arcade**, with a wide choice of video games in its 150 sq m.

The Gaumont cinema complex has 15 wide-screen theatres as well as a huge **IMAX screen** (programme on www.cinemasgaumontpathe.com).

La Légende de Buffalo Bill is a show based on the one Buffalo Bill produced on his European Tour over a century ago. Cowboys and Indians put on a rompin', stompin' Wild West spectacular complete with horses, bison and longhorn steer. Two evening performances; reservation recommended: tel. 01 60 45 71 00. Two price categories according to seating and type of meal (€71 adults, €57 children 3 to 11; or €59 adults, €45 children) including a cowboy-style dinner, drinks and a whole lot of hoopin' and hollerin'!

Seasonal activities are held at **Marina del Rey** between Disney Village and Disney's Hotel New York. See the whole scene from **PanoraMagique**, the world's largest captive balloon (€12 adults, €6 children), which rises to 100 m, weather permitting.

shopping

Shelf upon shelf of cuddly toys, racks and racks of Cinderella costumes, T-shirts and sweatshirts, Minnie headbands, funny hats, jars full of candy, Mickey Mouse mugs, paintboxes, moneyboxes, lollipops – take your shopping easy or you'll soon go into overload.

There are shops everywhere, in the parks, the hotels, in Disney Village, so once you've done all the rides and seen all the shows, you can, literally, shop till you drop.

The décor of all the stores is carefully themed to match their locations and each has its own character. It's well worth looking beyond the merchandise to examine the meticulous details of the walls and fittings.

SHOPPING SERVICE

- To save having to carry your purchases around all day, you can arrange to have them delivered directly to the Disney Store in Disney Village, where you can pick them up after 6 p.m., or to the boutique of your hotel, where they will be waiting for you from 8 p.m.

If you want to buy something without a Disney logo, you'll have to go to Val d'Europe (see p. 49) or Paris.

Disneyland Park

On your right hand as you enter Main Street U.S.A., the first shop you come to is **Bixby Brothers Men's Accessories**, which despite the name is full of Disney toys. The delightful **Ribbons & Bows Hat Shop** next door is outwardly an old-fashioned milliners, but filled inside with racks of enchanting baby clothes, many with Winnie the Pooh motifs.

At **Town Square Photography** on the opposite corner, you can stock up on films and other supplies. There's a fascinating display of antique cameras and daguerreotypes, and an old party-line phone which you can unhook to eavesdrop on the private conversations of the Main Street inhabitants.

shopping

Chocolate, marshmallow, lollipops and sweets are piled ceiling-high in the **Boardwalk Candy Palace**, which specializes in home-made fudge in mouthwatering flavours and sold in massive slabs. The décor is definitely worth a photo (note the glass columns filled with coloured boiled sweets).

Disney Clothiers Ltd is a gracious apartment converted into a shop selling clothes for all ages.

At **Main Street Motors**, why not pose for a souvenir photo by the vintage car of your dreams. Despite the name, it's a shop devoted to Disney-theme clothes and toys.

Harrington's Fine China and Porcelains houses **Glass Fantasies** (charming glass slippers) and **Disneyana Collectibles** (rare books, framed Disney "cellos" and lithographs).

On the other side of the street, as you head back towards Town Square, look into **Disney & Co.**, selling T-shirts and children's gifts and toys. Next door, **Lilly's Boutique** specializes in household articles and pretty bathroom fittings.

The Emporium is a large and splendid 19th-century department store, with a beautiful stained-glass cupola over the cash desk. Here you'll find clothes, toys, and a wide choice of souvenirs with Disney motifs.

Next to City Hall, **The Storybook Store** sells books in several languages, records and video tapes.

In Frontierland, the **Thunder Mesa Mercantile Building**, with its covered sidewalks of wooden planks and old shop signs, sells clothes, toys and accessories on a western theme: genuine stetsons, fringed leather jackets, sepia photos of Indian chiefs.

In Adventureland Bazar, the meandering boutique called **Les Trésors de Schéhérazade** is full of cuddly toys and fairytale dresses for budding Cinderellas.

The curious giraffe of **La Girafe Curieuse** is munching away at the branches of a tree growing in the middle of the shop. The theme is ecological: wooden toys, shells, stones, beads and feathers, "friends of nature" T-shirts and Disney toys.

Indiana Jones Adventure Outpost sells clothing and accessories on the Indiana Jones theme, bush hats for example. You'll find similar wares at the **Temple Traders Boutique**, near the entrance to the Indiana Jones ride.

shopping

Inside the pirates' fort, **Le Coffre du Capitaine** sells nautical novelties, jokey masks, swords and daggers, rubber spiders, and the indispensable hook for little pirates.

Treasures await in the Sleeping Beauty's castle: in a gem-studded cavern hewn out of the rock, cluttered with flasks and mysterious vials, **Merlin l'Enchanteur** is a shop for those of a scientific or esoteric bent: jewellery, medieval figurines, swords and decorative articles in crystal.

At the bottom of the right-hand castle ramp, Sleeping Beauty's three fairy godmothers reign over **La Confiserie des Trois Fées**, a sweetshop where lollipops grow on trees.

It's Christmas or some other holiday every day in **La Boutique du Château**, which displays a multitude of festive gifts arrayed on trees beneath a barrel-vaulted ceiling. A chipmunk, rabbits, an owl and other of the Sleeping Beauty's forest friends are sculpted on the ornate stone fireplace.

See the Seven Dwarfs' little beds, neatly lined up beneath the thatched roof of their cottage, **La Chaumière des Sept Nains**. Here you can buy games, toys, jewellery and clothes.

Geppetto's workshop, **La Bottega di Geppetto**, displays his workbench and the tools of his trade, together with all kinds of hand-carved wooden items, but it sells mainly items for babies and small children.

Toys, games and clothing for adults and children are on sale at **Sir Mickey's**, a pretty little shop with a giant beanstalk growing outside.

In Discoveryland, the dark blue walls of **Constellations** are scattered with stars, and astronomical instruments form part of the décor. The shop sells Disney character toys, clothing and other souvenirs. You'll recognize **Star Traders** by the radar on the roof. In the hi-tech interior of solar panels and grey metal, choose from Star Wars toys and gadgets and Disney sportswear.

Walt Disney Studios Park

At the entrance to the park, **Studio Photo** sells souvenirs, accessories and cameras.

On the other side of the courtyard, **Walt Disney Studios Store** is the biggest shop in the park; a statue of Mickey Mouse surfing across a roll of film takes centre stage. Here you'll find a vast selection of souvenirs on a

shopping

cinematic theme, ranging from soft toys to tea mugs.

On the left-hand side of Hollywood Boulevard, behind a film set depicting façades of American stores from the 1920s to the 1960s, **Legends of Hollywood** is part ancient Egypt, part surfing beach, part gas station! Items on sale range from beach mats to miniature Cadillacs, American State number plates, and replicas of the famous Oscar award.

You can hand your films in for developing at any of the stores mentioned above.

Comfortably cushioned inside the giant hat of the Sorcerer's Apprentice, **the Disney Animation Gallery**, sells collectors' items, figurines, cellos and other objects from the Walt Disney Classic Collection.

When you stagger out of the Rock 'n'Roller Coaster starring Aerosmith, come back down to earth in **Rock Around the Shop**; all the goods on sale have a connection with music.

Disney Village

The first thing that strikes you as you enter the gate is the spectacular ramp leading to the blue globe of **Planet Hollywood Disneyland Paris**. At

PIN TRADING

Calling all pin collectors! If you have any pins you want to swap, bring them to the resort and show them to the Cast Members wearing strips studded with pins. They might just have a treasure for your collection. Pins and strips are sold at special Pin Trading Stations in many of the shops; look out for limited editions, special issues and the new Stitch and Sweet Treats pins.

ground level, behind a wall set with the hand-prints of all your favourite movie stars, is the **Merch Shop**, a store where you can take your pick from the whole collection of Planet Hollywood clothing and accessories.

Further along, on the same side of the street, the **Buffalo Trading Company** behind its rustic wooden façade is full of Western-style souvenirs and clothes, Indian silver and turquoise jewellery, Tex-Mex food items, and genuine Aussie oilskin riding coats complete with adjustable saddle flap.

shopping

Carry on to the extraordinary **Rainforest Café** and its lush boutique featuring a talking tree, and a superb aquarium where the colourful fish negotiate an overhead tunnel. Here you can purchase tasteful T-shirts, accessories and toys on the theme of all things furry, hairy, feathery, scaly and slimy: jungle bugs, frogs, snakes, spiders and other creepy creatures of the rainforest.

On the other side of the street, **World of Toys** encompasses not only toys but also games, costumes for dressing up as Cinderella, Mulan, Peter Pan or the Sleeping Beauty, jewellery, Mickey Mouse lollipops and other sweets.

Next comes **Disney's Fashions** packed with fabulous sports gear (baseball shirts and so on), T-shirts and other clothes with Disney logos.

If you're looking for something rare (and expensive), call in at the **Disney Gallery** where you can invest in original "cellos" from animated films, bejewelled figurines of the Disney characters, high-quality ceramics and fine books.

The Disney Store sells clothes for all ages, and a wide variety of souvenirs and gifts.

La Vallée® Shopping Village

At Val d'Europe, a model town just a few minutes away from the resort, La Vallée Shopping Village is a long winding row of 75 chic boutiques selling prestigious brands of designer fashions, accessories, tableware and kitchenware at reduced prices, enabling you to save up to 50% on the previous year's collections. It is one of a chain of nine outlet shopping villages in Europe. Open seven days a week, Monday to Saturday 10 a.m.–7 p.m., Sunday 11 a.m.–7 p.m.

www.LaValleeVillage.com
www.chicoutletshopping.com

Close by, the Val d'Europe shopping centre is a vast and shiny mall with a huge Auchan hypermarket, department stores, boutiques and services (bank, restaurants, hairdressers, fitness centre, etc.), and the **Sea Life** aquarium, featuring touch pools, a mangrove swamp, a tropical lagoon and a shark academy, among many other marine mysteries.

Val d'Europe is one stop away from Marne-la-Vallée-Chessy on the RER, direction Paris. If you are staying in a resort hotel, ask the concierge to book you a seat on the door-to-door shuttle bus.

Dining out

The American accent is still strong in the resort's many restaurants, though a few concessions have been made to satisfy French tastes, notably in the wine department. Most have set menus or fixed price buffets; for a gourmet experience, book a table at Walt's – an American Restaurant, or the Blue Lagoon if you like fish.

Make your choice early in the day and reserve a table for lunch or dinner (tel. 01 60 30 40 50). Peak hours are noon–2.30 p.m. You could also head for one of the restaurants in Disney Village, which are quieter at lunch time. Picnics are not allowed in the park.

Menus and prices are posted in front of each restaurant in English and French. As they change frequently, we concentrate here on the type and décor of each establishment, rather than giving details of the food served there. Some restaurants have weekly or seasonal closing days.

Disneyland Park

On the west side of Main Street U.S.A., **Walt's – an American Restaurant** is sumptuously decorated with paintings and objets d'art from Walt Disney's personal collection. It's very chic, with something of a genteel drawing-room atmosphere, and the food is highly rated. Wine, beer and champagne are available. (Table service)

Casey's Corner sells excellent hot dogs and soft drinks in an atmosphere and setting dedicated to baseball. (Counter service)

Plaza Gardens Restaurant on the east side has seats for 300 inside and 100 more on the terrace. In a pretty setting resembling a Victorian summerhouse, choose from a generous display of roast or grilled meats, soups and salads, and scrumptious desserts. (Fixed-price buffet). Teatime with the characters every afternoon from 3 to 5.30 p.m.

There's an old-fashioned family atmosphere at **Victoria's Home-Style**

Dining out

SNACKS

If you feel peckish between meals, head for a food stall dotted around the various lands: they sell popcorn, candyfloss *(barbe à papa)*, toffee apples *(pommes d'amour)*, baked potatoes and other goodies, as well as cold beverages.

Restaurant, where you can sample light snacks. (Counter service)

Market House Deli specializes in freshly made, satisfying sandwiches, and melt-in-the-mouth brownies. If all the seats are taken you can carry your tray through to the back and sit at one of the tables in the Discovery Arcade. (Counter service)

Call at the **Gibson Girl Ice Cream Parlour** for a terrific Ben & Jerry's sundae or cornet. Those with a sweet tooth will enjoy brownies and muffins at the **Cookie Kitchen**, partitioned into cosy cubicles. Similar fare is served at the **Cable Car Bake Shop**. **The Ice Cream Company** is open in summer; **The Coffee Grinder** next door serves drinks and snacks.

The plushest place to be in Frontierland is the **Lucky Nugget Saloon**, providing from noon to 3 p.m. a fixed-price Tex-Mex buffet lunch, together with musical entertainment and Disney characters in cowboy costume.

Silver Spur Steakhouse is very classy; you can sample huge steaks grilled over a wood fire, and Tex-Mex dishes. Wine, beer and champagne available. It's worth visiting just to admire the sumptuous décor. (Table service)

Tex-Mex food – *fajitas, chili, quesadillas* – also stars in the **Fuente del Oro Restaurante**, a typical Mexican *cantina*. Everything is speedily served, and you can dine in the terracotta-paved patio by the ancient Maya fountain, or in the indoor dining room. (Counter service)

The **Last Chance Cafe** is an outlaw's hideaway with "Wanted" posters all over the walls. Light meals, meat sandwiches and takeaway snacks are served here. You can dine outside on the shady terrace, overlooking Big Thunder Mountain. (Counter service)

Cowboys and farmers join in the fun at the **Cowboy Cookout Barbecue**, in a huge barn near the Cotton-

Dining out

wood Creek Ranch. There are enough assorted tables and chairs to seat 650. The food is country-style: barbecued chicken, spare ribs and hamburgers, and sometimes the Cowhand Band provides rousing country and western music. (Counter service)

In Adventureland, all the glamour of the souk awaits in **Agrabah Café**, serving delectable North African dishes such as couscous, sticky syrup-laden pastries and mint tea. (Counter service)

During your boat ride in the Pirates of the Caribbean you'll see part of the **Blue Lagoon Restaurant** bathed in a cool moon glow. Sophisticated variations of fish and seafood dominate the menu, and wine, beer and champagne are served. (Table service).

The jungle-style **Hakuna Matata**, built to resemble an African mud hut, serves Mediterranean specialities. (Counter service)

On the waterfront, the **Café de la Brousse** is set in grass-thatched, palm-frond huts. Sandwiches, snacks and drinks. (Counter service)

Colonel Hathi's Pizza Outpost is a typical colonial-style mansion with an airy veranda overlooking a waterfall. A variety of pizzas and salads. (Counter service)

Children will love **Captain Hook's Galley**, aboard the galleon anchored in front of Skull Rock. Light refreshments may be savoured with drinks mixed by his faithful buccaneers behind the bar. Open only in summer. (Counter service)

In Fantasyland, in a cosy Alpine setting, **Au Chalet de la Marionnette** offers fast food such as hamburgers, chicken and chips. (Counter service)

A medieval banquet hall hung with Aubusson tapestries, the lovely **Auberge de Cendrillon** is a restaurant fit for a princess, complete with pumpkin-shaped carriage parked in the courtyard. Fine French tradition-

BREAKFAST WITH THE CHARACTERS

Give your children a big treat by breakfasting with Mickey Mouse and his friends. Bumper buffets are offered in the hotel restaurants or in the park itself, one hour before opening time, at *Walt's, an American Restaurant*. To book, see the concierge of your hotel.

Dining out

al cuisine is served in Cinderella's inn with some novelties such as *La Pantoufle de Cendrillon* (Cinderella's slipper) for dessert. Wine, beer and champagne available. (Table service)

Pizzeria Bella Notte offers pasta with a choice of sauces, and, naturally, pizzas. The setting is based on the Venetian trattoria of *Lady and the Tramp*. (Counter service)

For another taste of Italy, call for a delectable ice cream at **Fantasia Gelati**, next door, open March to November and on weekends in winter. (Counter service)

Sandwiches and light refreshments are served in **The Old Mill**, inspired by Disney's short film of the same name (1937). It's in a patio garden in front of Les Pirouettes du Vieux Moulin. (Counter service)

Anyone in desperate need of a British delicacy such as fish and chips or a chicken sandwich should set their sights on **Toad Hall Restaurant**, next to Peter Pan's Flight. Based on Kenneth Grahame's *The Wind in the Willows*, the setting is a typical English half-timbered country manor, with a proud portrait of Mr Toad in the library in the guise of the Laughing Cavalier. (Counter service)

HAPPY BIRTHDAY!

You can order a dazzling birthday cake in any of the restaurants in the hotels, Disney Village, Plaza Gardens or the other park restaurants with table service. Book at your hotel Information Desk or call at the restaurant itself at least two hours in advance.

In Discoveryland, hungry space travellers will find all the sustenance they need (hamburgers and chips) at the **Café Hyperion** in Videopolis, or in **Buzz Lightyear's Pizza Planet** hidden away behind Space Mountain. There's a play area to keep the children out of mischief while you enjoy your salad or pizza. (Counter service)

Walt Disney Studios Park

On the right-hand side of Hollywood Boulevard, behind a large film set representing the façades of real and imaginary nightclubs and restaurants, **En Coulisse** restaurant can seat 670 people on two floors, with a mezzanine overlooking all the action in the street down below. It serves

Dining out

pizzas, hamburgers, chickenburgers and salads. (Counter service)

To dine in the distinguished company of the greatest European and American movie stars – or at least with their photos – head for the **Rendez-vous des Stars** in Hollywood Studio. Along with other awards, one of the 26 Oscars won by Walt Disney is displayed in a showcase in this big Miami-style Art Deco restaurant serving European and international cuisine. (Buffet service)

La Terrasse is an open-sided, covered area with tables for two or four, where you can rest a while with a drink, or enjoy a snack from one of the many food stalls scattered around the park.

Festooned with a jumble of props and accessories (including a Jedi speeder bike), the **Backlot Express Restaurant** is designed to resemble the busy backstage area of a real production studio. Here you can choose from a wide selection of club and baguette sandwiches, quiches, salads and pastries. (Counter service).

The unusual **Café des Cascadeurs** is set inside a mobile production van of the type used by actors and stuntmen on location.

Disney Village

For a satisfying meal of grilled meats and fried potatoes, opt for the Chicago-style **Steakhouse**, reminiscent of the days of Al Capone. Sunday brunch with the Disney characters noon–3 p.m. Lunch daily (except Saturday) noon–3 p.m.; dinner 6–11 p.m. (Saturday to midnight).

Café Mickey overlooks the lake. Choose from a wide range of starters and main courses (like foie gras with a sauternes jelly, or rosemary honey pork spare ribs), and an eat-as-much-as-you-fancy dessert buffet.

Dripping with lush tropical vegetation and resounding with animal calls, the **Rainforest Café** will delight the children. Open noon–midnight.

The giant **McDonald's**, with its Commedia dell'Arte décor, has an attractive indoor play area to keep the kids out of mischief. Open daily 9 a.m.–midnight, Friday and Saturday to 1 a.m.

A typical American deli, **New York Style Sandwiches** serves bagels, big sandwiches and brownies (takeaway or served on the spot). Daily 11 a.m.–11 p.m., Saturday to midnight.

In typical 1950s style, **Annette's Diner** serves hamburgers, hot-dogs,

Dining out

sandwiches, salads and milkshakes. The waitresses zoom around on roller skates. Open daily noon–midnight, Saturday to 1 a.m.

King Ludwig's Castle is a turreted fantasy based on Neuschwanstein Castle in the Bavarian forest. Inside, the magnificent wood-panelled restaurant resembles Ludwig's throne room; the food is fit for a German king, including a Royal sauerkraut and Oktoberfest chicken, with an astounding variety of beer and wines.

On the third floor of **Billy Bob's Country Western Saloon**, enjoy a Tex-Mex buffet to live country music. Open daily 6.30–11.30 p.m. (snacks also served 6–11.30 p.m.)

The sparkling restaurant of the stars, **Planet Hollywood** finds its inspiration in Californian cuisine. Open daily 11.30 a.m.–1 a.m.

Hotels

Do try to spend several days at the Disneyland resort. You'll get the most out of it if you stay at a hotel on the spot and take advantage of the vast range of activities available to hotel guests.

Most hotels have rooms sleeping four people, and cabins at the self-catering Disney's Davy Crockett Ranch can sleep four to six. The six Disney hotels are within walking distance of the parks, and frequent yellow shuttle buses link them with the railway station. Pink buses serve the Disney-recommended hotels at Val de France and on the golf course, while those at Val d'Europe are just 5 minutes away by RER. However, the only way to get from Disney's Davy Crockett Ranch to the theme parks is by car, a 15-minute journey.

Disneyland Hotel
Standing majestically at the entrance to Disneyland Park, this luminous hotel in pink and white recalls the style of Florida and California resort hotels of the early 1900s. Service is elegant and refined, the décor luxurious, on a Disney theme. On request, Mickey Mouse, Minnie, Goofy, Pluto and other familiar friends will join guests for "Character breakfasts". *Indoor pool, fitness centre, playroom, video games room, shop (Galerie Mickey), two restaurants, bar. All rooms and suites with TV, telephone, air-conditioning, hair drier, minibar, safe, 24-hour room service, laundry service.*

Disney's Hotel New York
A combination of Manhattan skyscraper and East Side brown-stone, this superb hotel recalls New York of the 1930s. The furnishings and fittings are Art Deco, all on the Big Apple theme; even the table lamp is a model of the Empire State Building. *Convention Centre, indoor and outdoor pools, fitness centre, ladies' hairdresser, playroom, video games room, tennis courts, shop (New York Boutique), skating rink, two*

Hotels

restaurants, bar. All rooms and suites with TV, telephone, air-conditioning, hair drier, minibar, safe, 24-hour room service, laundry service.

Disney's Newport Bay Club

Designed in the grand tradition of the New England coastal resorts, this elegant hotel at the far end of Lake Disney has a definite yacht club feel about it, with reclining chairs looking out over the water. There's even a lighthouse. The décor is in jaunty navy and white, with the nautical theme carried through to the ships sailing over the bedroom curtains. *Convention Centre, indoor and outdoor pools, fitness centre, playroom, playground, video games room, shop (Bay Boutique), two restaurants, two bars. All rooms and suites with TV, telephone, air-conditioning, minibar, safe, room service, laundry service.*

Disney's Sequoia Lodge

Back to nature in this rustic timber and stone complex in a forest setting, the unmistakable scent of fir trees fills the air. The rooms are decorated like

In the pink: a stay in the Disneyland Hotel is the ultimate in luxury.

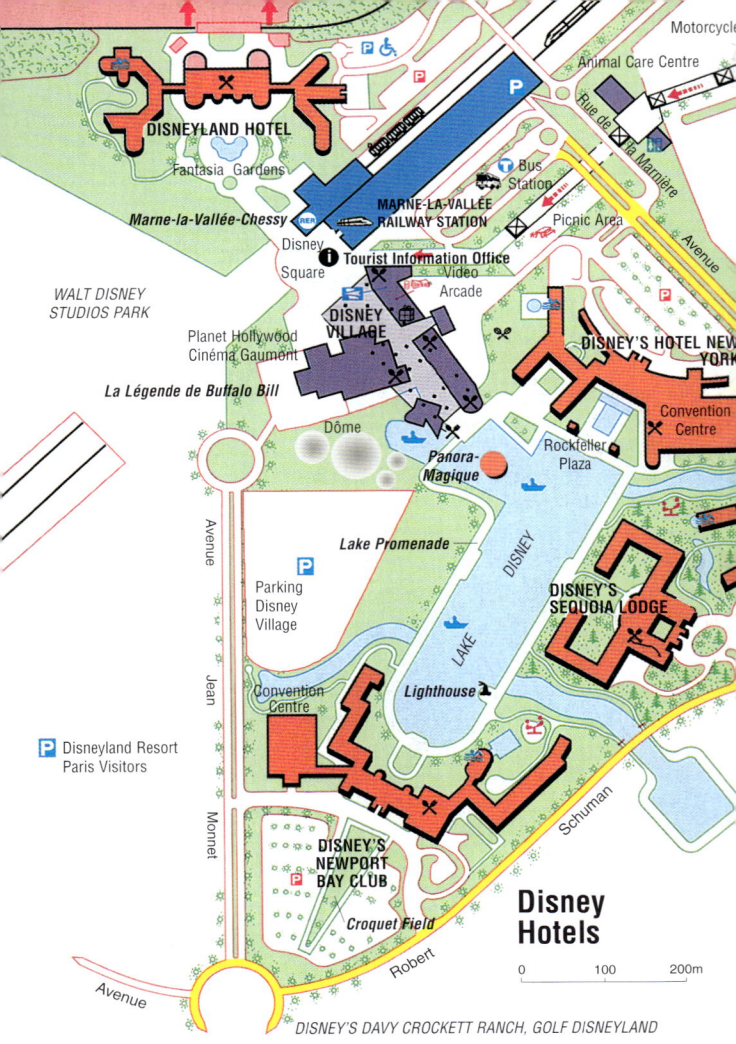

Hotels

hunting lodges, with solid wood furniture and patchwork quilts. *Indoor and outdoor pools, fitness centre, video games room, playroom, playground, shop (Northwest Passage), two restaurants, bar. All rooms with TV, telephone, air-conditioning, minibar in most of the Montana rooms, suites, laundry service.*

Disney's Hotel Cheyenne

Fourteen buildings along Desperado Street and Rio Grande house the Wild West bedrooms, with bunk beds for the children and lampshades of buffalo hide. *Video games room, playroom, playground (Indian village with pony rides), General Store, restaurant, country music in saloon. All rooms with TV, telephone, ceiling fan, laundry facilities.*

Disney's Hotel Santa Fe

America's Southwest comes to life in this pueblo village set along the banks of the Rio Grande. Furnishings in warm ochre and terracotta tones. *Video games room, playroom, playground, shop (Trading Post), Tex-Mex restaurant, bar. All rooms with TV, telephone, ceiling fan, laundry facilities.*

Disney's Davy Crockett Ranch

Natural woodlands provide the perfect setting for this pioneer-style campground. Each log cabin sleeps six, with living room, kitchen, bedroom, bathroom and a cleaning service. *Cycling and jogging tracks, playroom, playground, video games room, farm with pony rides, mini-zoo, indoor pool, archery, tennis courts, kart track, bicycle hire, food shop (Alamo Trading Post), restaurant, bar. All bungalows with TV, telephone, picnic tables, barbecue grills. Equipped tent and caravan sites, laundry facilities, heated bathroom facilities.*

Four **Disney-recommended hotels** are grouped close together on a wooded site near a lake at Val de France, while another is right on the course, overlooking the links. All are served by shuttle bus, a 10-minute journey from the park.

Holiday Inn

The perfect choice for families with young children, this big manor-style hotel is decorated throughout on a circus theme. Rooms (called "Kids' Rooms") sleep up to four, with one double bed and a special children's corner with two bunk beds, TV and video games. The bar is called *Le Funambule* (The Tight-rope Walker); the restaurant, *Le Saltimbanque* (The Acrobat), offers traditional French and international cuisine. In fine weather you can dine outside. Breakfast is a hot and cold buffet. *Indoor pool, with play area and fitness centre, video games room, shop, restaurant, bar. All rooms with TV, video games, Internet access, telephone, safe, hair drier, air-conditioning, room service, laundry service.*

Thomas Cook's Explorers Hotel

Overlooking the lake, this hotel forms a rampart around the fortified castle of Sir Archibald de Bacle. The rooms and public areas are furnished on a nautical theme, decorated with objects garnered from the Seven Seas. The *Captain's Library* restaurant, with a play area, serves traditional European cuisine, while the *Plantation Restaurant* is more international (the Continental buffet breakfast is served here). For a quick meal, opt for *Marco's Pizza Parlour*, where you can dine on the spot or buy a takeaway. *The Wreck of the Seven Seas Raider*, with its bridge, cabins, gangways and slide gives access to the *Secret Lagoon* pool, and there's plenty more to amuse the kids at *Scally Wagg's Jungle Adventure* (indoor adventure playground) and *Harry's Action Zone* (video games). *Indoor adventure playground, indoor pool, video games room, shop, three restaurants, three bars. All rooms with TV, video games, Internet access, safe, hair drier, ceiling fan.*

Hôtel Kyriad

In a woodland setting, the Kyriad is built in the traditional style of the Brie region; the airy rooms can sleep up to four, with one double and two bunk beds. Traditional French cuisine, Continental buffet breakfast. *Outdoor playground, shop, restaurant, two bars. All rooms with TV, telephone, air-conditioning, hair drier, tea and coffee-making facilities.*

Vienna International Dream Castle Hotel

Even the beds are king-size in this hotel where every guest is treated like royalty. Enjoy the buffet in the *Mus-*

keteers restaurant and drink a magic potion in the *Excalibur* bar overlooking the gardens, lake and hills, keep fit in the *Torture Chamber*, or go and swim in the *Dragon's Lagoon*. *All rooms with bathroom, telephone, satellite TV, radio, Internet access, video games, minibar, safety-deposit box, hair drier, air-conditioning. 3 restaurants, bar, room service, Disney shop, outdoor play area, indoor children's corner, heated indoor pool, fitness room.*

Radisson SAS Hotel

On the edge of the Disneyland Golf Course, a stylish hotel with standard and family rooms, and suites. *Restaurant, rôtisserie, bar, Wellness & Fitness Centre with swimming pool, sauna, steam bath, massage; 12 meeting rooms, free broadband.*

In nearby Val d'Europe, you can stay in the following **Disney-associated hotels** and **residence**. They are 3 km away from the theme parks by car, 5 minutes by RER train. (Disney also recommends a number of hotels in Paris and the Marne-la-Vallée region, some on the RER route, but handier if you come by car.)

Hôtel Elysée Val d'Europe

A large, modern, three-star hotel in "grand boulevard" style. Rooms sleep up to four, with one double and two single beds. Traditional French cuisine in La Brasserie; Continental buffet breakfast. *Playground, video games room, restaurant, bar. All rooms with television, telephone, minibar, safe, hair drier, air-conditioning. Suites available. Room service breakfast only. Garage, day nursery.*

Adagio City Aparthotel

This residence of self-catering apartments is ideal for families who want to feel at home. Two or three room apartments sleep from four to seven people. Kitchenette with electric hob, fridge, microwave oven and dishwasher. Separate bathroom and toilet. Some apartments are duplex. Bed-linen and towels are provided, and breakfast is included. *Heated outdoor pool. Refundable deposit of €200 required on arrival (payable by cheque or credit card only). At extra cost: telephone, TV, safe, babysitting, house-keeping, detergents, covered car park, launderette, cot, high chair.*

Golf Disneyland

Five kilometres (3 miles) southeast of the parks, the championship course was designed by Ronald Fream of California. It's open all year round except Christmas Day and New Year's Day, first tee-off between 8.30 and 9 a.m. according to season.

This superb 27-hole course is suitable for players of all levels. It is divided into three 9-hole segments (each par 36) allowing golfers to play three different 18-hole courses. Minimum level of game required: 53.5. Shoes, clubs and electric golf carts can be rented. The practice area can hold 40 people, and there's a 600-sq-m putting green in the shape of a Mickey Mouse head. The clubhouse has a restaurant, a pro shop, a meeting hall, TV room and changing rooms.

For information and reservations, tel. 01 60 45 68 90. Driving directions: A4 motorway, direction Metz/Nancy; exit 14, follow signs marked "Disneyland Paris Golf/ Magny-le-Hongre.

The hard facts

Getting to Disneyland

By train. Several European cities are linked directly with Marne-la-Vallée by TGV, Thalys and Eurostar trains. From Paris, the regional express train, RER, line A, runs to Marne-la-Vallée-Chessy. Trains are frequent and the journey takes just over half an hour. Different trains run on the same line: make sure you get on the one going all the way to Chessy, the terminus. A one-way ticket from the centre of Paris costs € 6.45.

By air. The nearest airports are Orly and Roissy-Charles de Gaulle, both linked by VEA shuttle bus to Disneyland. Tickets are sold on board, and can be paid for in cash or by credit card (single fare, adult: €17, children 3–11 €13). On departure, allow at least 2.5 hours before your plane leaves for transfer and check-in.

By road. From England or northern Europe, take the A1, then after Roissy airport turn east onto the A104 (Francilienne) to join the A4, dir. Metz at Marne-la-Vallée. **Exit 14 "Parcs Disney" for parks and hotels**; exit 13 Provins/Serris for Disney's Davy Crockett Ranch (white signs).

The hard facts

Animals
Pets must be left at the Animal Care Center for the whole length of your stay. Tattoo and veterinary certificate of good health required. Guide dogs are allowed into most attractions.

Babies
In the Disneyland Park, the Baby Care Center at the end of Main Street has facilities for warming bottles, feeding and nappy-changing. Pushchairs can be rented at Town Hall Terrace, on your left after you pass through the turnstile (refundable deposit), and in the Walt Disney Studios Park, to the right of the entrance to Front Lot. In the hotels, bottle warmers, sterilizers, baby baths and various other accessories are available on request to the housekeeper.

Baggage
Bags can be left at Guest Storage (at the right-hand entrance to each park, but the one at the Studios park is not always open). The fee is €2.50 for small bags, €4 for suitcases. If you have booked into a hotel and arrive in the morning, you can leave your luggage with the hotel concierge. The same goes if you are leaving in the afternoon or evening (hotel rooms must be vacated by 11 a.m.). The lockers beneath Main Street Station are closed because of government security measures.

Car Parks
For Disney hotel guests and for those staying at Disney's Davy Crockett Ranch, parking is free at the hotel and at the Disneyland public car park. Visitors parking: €5 per day for motorbikes, €8 for cars, €13 for campervans. There's a petrol station near the Santa Fe hotel. A four-storey Vinci car park in Art Deco style serves Disney Village (between the village and the Studios park).

Climate
The weather in Marne-la-Vallée is unpredictable. July and August are hot; May/June, September/October pleasant; winter months can be cold, wet and windy. The region tends to be showery whatever the season.

Clothing
Mickey likes everyone to be neat and pretty. Be casual but don't go barefooted or bare-chested. Make sure you wear comfortable shoes.

The hard facts

Electricity
The voltage in the hotels is 220 V; plugs have two round prongs. Adaptors are on sale in the hotel shops. Kettles and irons can be supplied on request to the housekeeper.

Emergency Supplies
A very limited selection of toiletries is available in the hotel and park boutiques. You will find a better supply, including disposable nappies, toothpaste, etc. in the railway station, in the small Casino supermarket (it closes at 7 p.m.) It also has a few shelves of plastic-wrapped sandwiches, fruit tarts, yoghurts, biscuits, crisps, chocolate, fruit, bottles of mineral water and other drinks.

Entry ticket
One-day tickets are available for one park, either Disneyland or Walt Disney Studios. To visit both parks you need a Park Hopper ticket, available for 1 to 5 days, which do not have to be consecutive. Entry is free for children aged 3 and under. Tickets are valid for one year (see expiry date stamped on the back). Till April 2, 2009, hotel accommodation and park entry is free for children under 12 if you book a package. For current prices and special offers, see the website www.disneylandparis.com.

There are three annual passes: Francilien giving access on 300 days per year; Fantasy valid for a year except for 30 specific days; and Dream for unlimited access all year round. The Fantasy and Dream passes also include free parking, reductions in boutiques and some hotels, and other benefits; all three offer reductions in the restaurants. They can be bought at the park entrances, at Disney Stores and various other large stores in France, as well as on www.disneylandparis.com. A normal 1-day ticket can be exchanged for an annual passport by paying the difference the day of your visit: enquire at the **Annual Passport Office** in Discoveryland.

First Aid
A fully equipped centre is located just beside Plaza Gardens Restaurant in the Disneyland Park, and to the right of the entrance to Front Lot in Walt Disney Studios Park.

Guided tours/Hortitours
To appreciate fully the architecture of the parks, take a guided tour. Tickets

for standard tours (2 h Disneyland Park, 1 h Walt Disney Studios) are available at the main entrance, City Hall and Studio Services. VIP tours can be arranged for private groups. If you're interested in gardens, enquire about special Hortitours at City Hall.

Hours

The parks are normally open 10 a.m. to 7, 8, 9 or 10 p.m. in winter, from 9 a.m. to 11 p.m. in summer. Some hotels offer Extra Magic Hours outside the usual times, enabling you to avoid the crush at the gates.

Information

See the Guest Relations hosts at City Hall in Disneyland Park, or at Studio Services in Walt Disney Studios Park, or call 0825 30 60 30 (no. indigo, €0.15/min) for enquiries.

Lost Children, Lost Property

If you lose your child in the Disneyland Park, call at Lost Children, located inside the First Aid centre, and in the Walt Disney Studios Park, at the right-hand side of the entrance to Front Lot. For lost property, enquire at the right-hand entrance to either of the parks.

Mail

Post boxes are scattered throughout the parks and at the hotel receptions. The mail is collected daily. The post office, just inside the entrance to the Chessy-Marne-la Vallée railway station, is open seven days a week, and you can also buy postage stamps at stores in the parks and the hotels.

Money

All the rides inside the parks are free, but you'll need money for meals, snacks, purchases, photographs and coin-operated video games. Prices are given in euros (€). Cash points are located in Liberty and Discovery arcades, Disney Village and the hotels. Money can be changed at hotel reception desks, the post office, and American Express offices in the parks.

If you're staying in a resort hotel (except Santa Fe and Cheyenne) and pay with a major credit card, you'll be given a personal charge card which you can use everywhere except Planet Hollywood, Rainforest Café, McDonald's, Gaumont cinema, PanoraMagique, Lucie Saint-Claire hairdressing salon and the snack stalls. This system enables you to pay for practically everything on one bill at the end of your stay. The charge card can be used until 11 a.m. on the day of your departure.

Newspapers

For those who want to keep in touch with the real world, major European newspapers are sold in the hotel boutiques and at the kiosk in the station.

Photos

Flash photography is not allowed in any attraction. Good photo points are signposted. You can buy supplies at Town Hall Photography (Disneyland Park) or Studio Photo (Walt Disney Studios Park) where, for a special souvenir, you can have your picture taken and incorporated into a scene from one of your favourite animated films. Digital photos can be printed here, at the Kiosk Kodak.

Photos are automatically taken at Space Mountain, Big Thunder Mountain and Rock'n' Roller Coaster starring Aerosmith; they are available for purchase at the end of the ride.

Picnics

Food or drink must not be brought into the parks. There's a picnic area outside, between the visitors' car park and railway station. There are plenty of drinking fountains around the parks, generally near the toilets.

Queues

To avoid them, try to visit Disneyland early in the week, when it is less crowded. In peak season, make sure you're at the entrance at least 30 minutes before opening time. At the most popular rides, signs inform you as to the length of time you'll have to wait. The best time to visit them is first thing in the morning, during the afternoon parade, or in the evening. The Fastpass (see p. 5) will help you gain time. The quietest time of year is September to April, except for Christmas and during school holidays.

Parents with children too small for certain rides can benefit from the **Baby Switch** service. One parent takes the ride while the other looks after the children, then they change places and the other parent can take the ride without having to go to the start of the queue. See the Cast Members at the entrance to the ride.

Hot tip: guests staying at Disney's Newport Bay Club, Disney's Sequoia Lodge, Disney's Hotel Cheyenne or Disney's Hotel Santa Fe can take

The hard facts

breakfast in Fantasyland, an hour before the park opens, at no extra charge. This enables you to be among the first in line when Peter Pan's Flight opens. For more details, see your hotel concierge.

Re-admittance

If you want to leave the theme park, get the back of your hand stamped (it's invisible) and you'll be re-admitted as long as you have your entry ticket.

Safety

Space Mountain, Big Thunder Mountain, Star Tours, Indiana Jones™ et le Temple du Péril, Autopia and Rock 'n'Roller Coaster starring Aerosmith are not advised for guests with heart, back or neck problems, and Dumbo, Orbitron and Autopia are out of the question for children under 1 year old. Height restrictions are imposed for certain rides.

Security

Because of government security measures, bags may be searched at the main gates to the parks. The area between the station and parks is patrolled by police on horseback.

Special needs

Wheelchairs can be hired at Town Hall Terrace or near the entrance to the Walt Disney Studios Park for a nominal fee plus refundable deposit. The *Special Services Guest Guide*, a useful brochure for disabled visitors, is available at City Hall and Studio Services, and at the reception of the on-site hotels. Park maps in Braille are available in English and French at City Hall for a small refundable deposit. Cast members conversant in sign language wear a badge marked LSF. Guided tours in sign language must be booked four weeks ahead.

VAT Refund

If you live outside the EU and spend more than € 175 on purchases during any one stay, you can claim a partial refund of the sales tax. Take your receipts to your Disneyland hotel boutique, City Hall or the Disney Village shops, and you will be given the appropriate customs form.

What's on

To check on the shows at Disney Village, see www.disneylandparis.com, click on Disney Village and the "Now Showing" page.

Index

Adagio City Aparthotel 62
Adventure Isle 21–23
Adventureland 21–23
Agrabah Café 52
Alice's Curious Labyrinth 26
Annette's Diner 54–55
Animagique 36–37
Annual Passport Office 66
Armageddon Special Effects 42
Art of Disney Animation 37–38
Astroport Services Interstellaires 31
Au Chalet de la Marionnette 52
Auberge de Cendrillon 52–53
Autopia 31
Backlot 42–43
Backlot Express Restaurant 54
Ben Gunn's Cave 23
Big Thunder Mountain 19
Billy Bob's Country Western Saloon 44, 55
Birthdays 53
Bixby Brothers Men's Accessories 45
Blanche-Neige et les Sept Nains 25
Blue Lagoon Restaurant 52
Boardwalk Candy Palace 46
Boot Hill 19–20
Bottega di Geppetto 47
Boutique du Château 47

Breakfast with the characters 52
Buffalo Bill, la Légende de 44
Buffalo Trading Company 48
Buzz Lightyear Laser Blast 30–31
Buzz Lightyear's Pizza Planet 53
Cabane des Robinson 21
Cable Car Bake Shop 51
Café de la Brousse 52
Café des Cascadeurs 54
Café Hyperion 53
Café Mickey 54
Captain Hook's Galley 52
Carrousel de Lancelot 26
Cars: Quatre Roues Rallye 37
Casey Jr. le Petit Train du Cirque 27
Casey's Corner 50
Catastrophe Canyon 41
Chaparral Stage 20
Château de la Belle au Bois Dormant 25
Chaumière des Sept Nains 47
CinéMagique 39
City Hall 15
Coffee Grinder 51
Coffre du Capitaine 47
Colonel Hathi's Pizza Outpost 52
Confiserie des Trois Fées 47
Constellations 47
Cookie Kitchen 51
Cowboy Cookout Barbecue 51–52

Critter Corral 20
Crush's Coaster 37
CyberSpace Mountain 40
Dapper Dan's Hair Cuts 16
Discovery Arcade 16
Discoveryland 29–31
Disney & Co. 46
Disney Animation Gallery 48
Disney Channel Cyber Space 40
Disney Clothiers Ltd. 46
Disney Gallery 49
Disney Store 49
Disney Village 44, 48–49, 54–55
Disney's Davy Crockett Ranch 60
Disney's Fashions 49
Disney's Hotel Cheyenne 60
Disney's Hotel New York 56–57
Disney's Hotel Santa Fe 60
Disney's Newport Bay Club 57
Disney's Sequoia Lodge 57–60
Disneyana Collectibles 46
Disneyland Hotel 56
Disneyland Park 11–31, 45–47, 50–53
Disneyland Railroad 16
Dôme 44
Dumbo the Flying Elephant 26
Emporium 46
En Coulisse 53–54

70

Index

Excalibur 25
Fantasia Gelati 53
Fantasyland 25–27
Fastpass 7
Flying Carpets over Agrabah 37
Front Lot 33
Frontierland 19–20
Fuente del Oro Restaurante 51
Galerie de la Belle au Bois Dormant 25
Gaumont cinema 44
Gibson Girl Ice Cream Parlour 51
Girafe Curieuse 46
Glass Fantasies 46
Golf Disneyland 63
Grand Canyon Diorama 16
Guided Tours 66–67
Hakuna Matata 52
Harrington's Fine China and Porcelains 46
Holiday Inn 60–61
Hollywood Boulevard 33
Hollywood Studio 39–41
Honey, I Shrunk the Audience 30
Hortitours 66–67
Hôtel Elysée Val d'Europe 62
Hôtel Kyriad 61
Hurricane's 44
Ice Cream Company 51
Indiana Jones Adventure Outpost 46
Indiana Jones™ and the Temple of Péril 21
It's a Small World 27
King Ludwig's Castle 55
La Terrasse 54
La Vallée® Shopping Village 49
Last Chance Cafe 51
Legends of Hollywood 48
Legends of the Wild West 19
Liberty Arcade 15–16
Lilly's Boutique 46
Lucky Nugget Saloon 51
Mad Hatter's Tea Cups 26
Main Street Motors 46
Main Street, U.S.A. 15–17
March Hare Refreshments 26
Marina del Rey 44
Market House Deli 51
McDonald's 54
Merch Shop 48
Merlin l'Enchanteur 47
Mystères du Nautilus 29–30
New York Style Sandwiches 54
Nex Game Arcade 44
Old Mill 53
Orbitron 31
PanoraMagique 44
Parades 17
Passage Enchanté d'Aladdin 21
Pays des Contes de Fées 27
Peter Pan's Flight 26
Phantom Manor 19
Pin Trading 48
Pirates of the Caribbean 23
Pirates' Beach 23
Pirouettes du Vieux Moulin 27
Pizzeria Bella Notte 53
Planet Hollywood 48, 55
Plaza Gardens Restaurant 50
Pocahontas Indian Village 20
Radisson SAS Hotel 62
Rainforest Café 49, 54
Rendez-vous des Stars 54
Ribbons & Bows Hat Shop 45
Rivers of the Far West 20
Rock Around the Shop 48
Rock'n'Roller Coaster starring Aerosmith 42
Rustler Roundup Shootin' Gallery 20
Sea Life aquarium 49
Silver Spur Steakhouse 51
Sir Mickey's 47
Space Mountain – Mission II 29
Sports Bar 54
Star Tours 31
Star Traders 47
Steakhouse 54
Stitch Live 39
Storybook Store 46
Street theatre 39
Studio 1 33
Studio Photo 47
Studio Services 33
Studio Tram Tour 40–41
Stunt Show Spectacular 42–43

71

Index

Tanière du Dragon 25
Temple Traders Boutique 46
Thomas Cook's Explorers Hotel 61
Thunder Mesa Mercantile Building 46
Toad Hall Restaurant 53
Toon Studio 36–38
Town Square 15
Town Square Photography 45
Trésors de Schéhérazade 46
The Twilight Zone Tower of Terror 40
Val d'Europe 49, 62
Victoria's Home-Style Restaurant 50–51
Videopolis 31
Vienna International Dream Castle Hotel 61–62
Voyages de Pinocchio 25–26
Walt Disney Studios Park 33–43, 47–48, 53–54
Walt Disney Studios Store 47–48
Walt Disney Television Studios 39
Walt's – an American Restaurant 50
World of Toys 49

Text:	Barbara Ender-Jones
Design:	Guy Minder
Layout:	Alain Piccard
Maps:	© Michelin, from the map-guide Euro Disney Resort Authorization No 93-477; JPM Publications
Photography:	© Disney, p. 30 Barbara Ender

© DISNEY All characters and attractions referred to in this book are the property of THE WALT DISNEY COMPANY. All rights reserved. Among the numerous registered trademarks of The Walt Disney Company referred to in this book, the principal ones are as follows: Disneyland® Resort Paris, "Audio-Animatronics"®. We would like to thank Press Relations of Disneyland Resort Paris for helping us keep this guide up to date.

Copyright © 2009, 1993 by JPM Publications SA
12, avenue William-Fraisse, 1006 Lausanne, Switzerland
http://www.jpmguides.com/ — information@jpmguides.com
All rights reserved. No part of this book may be reproduced or transmitted in any form or by any means, electronic or mechanical, including photocopying, recording or by any information storage and retrieval system without permission in writing from the publisher.

Every effort has been made to ensure the accuracy of the information contained in this guide, but attractions, shops, restaurants and services are always subject to change. They are sometimes closed for refurbishment, and some operate on a seasonal basis. Therefore, neither JPM Publications SA nor its client can be held liable for any factual error of this kind.
Printed in Switzerland – Weber/Bienne – 10067.00.5288 – Edition 2009